How to Raise and Train a
BASSET HOUND

By ARTHUR LIEBERS
and
DOROTHY HARDY

Distributed in the U.S.A. by T.F.H. Publications, Inc., 211 West Sylvania Avenue, P.O. Box 27, Neptune City, N.J. 07753; in England by T.F.H. (Gt. Britain) Ltd., 13 Nutley Lane, Reigate, Surrey; in Canada by Clarke, Irwin & Company, Clarwin House, 791 St. Clair Avenue West, Toronto 10, Ontario; in Southeast Asia by Y. W. Ong, 9 Lorong 36 Geylang, Singapore 14; in Australia and the south Pacific by Pet Imports Pty. Ltd., P.O. Box 149, Brookvale 2100, N.S.W., Australia.
Published by T.F.H. Publications, Inc. Ltd., The British Crown Colony of Hong Kong.

ACKNOWLEDGMENTS

Pictures were taken by Heyer of Three Lions, Inc., with the cooperation of Mrs. Dorothy Hardy, Hubertus Kennel, East Meadow, Long Island, New York.

ISBN 0-87666-240-8

Contents

The Basset certainly cannot be called "beautiful," but his gentle disposition and comic ways make him a delightful pet.

1. The Basset — Comedian and Hunter

Cleo, the famed Basset of the TV screen, has brought national attention to the sad-eyed, long-eared hounds who have been described as being half a dog high and two dogs long. The Basset seems to be a natural comedian. It is as if he realizes he will never win any canine beauty prizes and so makes up in character and disposition for what he lacks in looks.

While many Bassets lead languid lives as placid, loyal house pets, the Basset has a long history as a hunting breed. For many centuries the Basset was bred in France and Belgium as the hunting dog of the royal families. For the fat or somewhat lazy hunter, the rather slow-moving Basset is the ideal companion in the field. Descended from the Bloodhound, the Basset has a good nose and is not far behind his ancestor in scenting ability. His short legs make him a good dog for hunting in thick cover. Foxes, rabbits and pheasants are his "meat" in the field. He is a steady trailer and habitually gives plenty of "tongue" so that he can be followed even when he is invisible in the brush. With training he is a good "coon dog" and can work on pheasants and other birds.

The Basset is a sociable dog. Used to hunting in packs, he is well able to get along with other dogs and will lavish affection on a person who treats him kindly. While he is somewhat a one-man dog, he will tolerate other members of the family and will be good with children. If you have a cat or birds in the house, the Basset will accept them as family members.

His disposition is good natured. Around the house he is satisfied to stay on his bed or on a favorite spot on the carpet most of the time—or on a piece of furniture, if it is allowed. He's not the type of dog to rush over and greet visitors by jumping on them. His characteristic approach to a stranger is a slow amble, a sociable sniff and a return to whatever he was or wasn't doing. Even as a puppy, the Basset usually isn't destructive. He is highly adaptable to training, learning quickly. While he may do things slowly, he's fairly reliable once he has absorbed his training.

THE BASSET'S FAMILY TREE

Dog experts don't agree among themselves about the origin of the Basset. It's generally accepted that Bassets are descended from dogs bred by the monks of St. Hubert's monastery in France during the 6th century. However, some trace the line back to dogs that were brought from Constantinople during the Crusades.

The breed has always been very much as it is today. Early writers have described black and tan dogs with low bodies, large heads, long ears, a loud, melodious "bay" and a gentle disposition.

Actually there is no such dog as a "Basset." The word itself means low-slung and was used by the French to designate any hunting hound dog that was less than 16 inches tall. As the hounds bred at St. Hubert's spread over France, they mated with many types of local hounds. These low hounds appeared in varied colors, some with straight legs, others with the crooked front legs that are characteristic of the modern Basset.

During the 15th century, these hounds were imported into England and, according to some authorities, were crossed with Bloodhounds. Thus the Basset acquired the deep-set eyes and wrinkled face. Over many generations the English and French Bassets developed along slightly different lines, the English dog becoming larger, heavier and less active than his French counterpart.

For the next few hundred years there was no true Basset breed—no dogs whose offspring would bear the characteristics of the parents and carry them down to the succeeding generations. In the late 1800's in France, however, two breeders, Count Le Couteul de Canteleu and Monsieur Lane, set out to develop a pure Basset strain. By selective breeding they each developed a true breed of Basset. The Lane dogs had large round eyes and a broad skull; the Count's dogs had the long-faced, sad look that is presently desirable and somewhat straighter and stronger legs than the Lane breed. The Le Couteul strain was brought to England, and while there are no early records, most of today's Bassets probably descended from dogs from the Count's kennels.

Although the Basset's history as a hunter goes back many centuries, his history as a show dog is fairly recent. The first Basset to be shown in England was imported from France and exhibited in 1875. It wasn't until 10 years later that a Basset was registered with the American Kennel Club and the Basset Hound Club of America was not formed until 1935.

2. Selecting Your Basset

So you're out to buy a Basset! Your first consideration should be to get a dog that is 100 per cent Basset, not one that is a mixture of Basset and one of the other hounds. If the dog is not purebred, even though the puppy may look like a Basset, the grown dog may not have the desirable Basset traits.

A purebred Basset will be the offspring of parents who are registered with the American Kennel Club or the Field Dog Stud Book. Even if you are primarily interested in a Basset as a pet or as a hunting dog and don't care about his papers, it is worth while to spend the few extra dollars for a purebred dog. A reputable kennel, pet shop or breeder can be relied on to sell dogs honestly.

It may not be too easy to find a desirable Basset puppy. There are only about 3,000 purebred Bassets registered in the United States—the dog is about 30th from the top in popularity among the 114 breeds that are officially recognized. Watch the dog advertisements in your newspaper and the ads in the dog magazines.

If there is a dog show in your vicinity, you will probably find a few Bassets entered and the exhibitors may have dogs for sale, or can suggest a source for your puppy.

MALE OR FEMALE?

Whether you choose a male or female Basset is up to you. With a non-aggressive breed like this, you needn't pick a female because you think the male may be too rough or hard to manage. On the other hand, the female is not too much trouble around the house the two times a year that she's in season. Most Bassets are good mothers, and if you intend to breed your dog, you can rely on her to do most of the work in giving birth and feeding the young puppies.

A HEALTHY PUPPY

You do want a healthy puppy. Normally, puppies are offered for sale when they are about six to eight weeks old. At that age, Bassets are quite a bit plumper than other puppies and they are beginning to have the typical Basset appearance.

Even the happiest Basset looks sad and mournful.

Even as a puppy the Basset is not a "ball of fire." But the puppy should be fairly active and show good coordination of his legs. His eyes should be clear and his coat in good condition. Any blotches on his skin are a bad sign. Check the dog's eyes and ears for any pus-like discharge and pass him over if his eyes or ears are running. A running nose or a very dry nose can also be a danger sign in a young puppy. Look at his teeth and gums and make sure they are not bleeding or malformed.

It is always wise to make your purchase subject to the approval of a veterinarian. The seller will usually allow you eight hours in which to take the puppy to a vet to have his health checked. Arrive at a clear agreement with the seller on what happens if the vet rejects the puppy. It should be understood whether rejection means you get your money back or merely the choice of another puppy.

THE BASSET'S PAPERS

If you are new to the dog world, the business of pedigrees, registration, and so forth can be pretty confusing. Basically, it's pretty much like this: each purebred dog is registered in the stud book for his breed. Then, in turn, his children can be registered, carrying on the line. In order for a dog to be eligible for registration, both his parents must have been registered.

The pedigree is a tracing of the dog's family tree. The breeder may have the pedigrees of the dog's parents and may make out a copy for you. Or, you can write to the American Kennel Club once your dog has been registered and ask for a pedigree. The fee depends on how many generations back you want the pedigree traced. In addition to giving the ancestors of your dog, the pedigree will show whether there are any champions or dogs that have won obedience degrees in his lineage. If you are planning selective breeding, the pedigree is also helpful to enable you to find other Bassets that have the same general family background.

Most purebred dogs are registered in the stud books of the A.K.C., although many owners of hounds and other sporting dogs prefer to register them in the Field Dog Stud Book. Some breeds are registered with the United Kennel Club.

Bassets are very sociable, getting along well with other dogs, cats, birds and people.

HOW TO REGISTER YOUR BASSET

As a rule, the puppy you buy has not been registered as an individual, but the breeder has probably registered the litter. Unless he has done this, you cannot register your puppy with the American Kennel Club. Both the puppy's parents must have been registered as purebred Bassets too. An unregistered dog cannot qualify for dog show awards or for obedience degrees and its offspring will be less valuable.

To register with the A.K.C., obtain an Application for Registration from the seller who will fill in the lines on the form that transfers ownership to you. The form should also bear the signature of the owner of the dam (mother in dog-language). You must now choose a name of 25 letters or less for your dog. You cannot use a name which is already being used by another dog of the same breed, nor can you name the dog after a living person without his written permission, or after a registered kennel without permission of the owner. (Unlike people, dogs are not generally called by the name that appears on their birth certificates. Mr. Lazybones of Utopia might be called "Mike" in his private life. In the dog world, the name that is commonly used is the "call name"; his official title is the registered name.) Then you mail the completed and signed application to the American Kennel Club, 221 Fourth Avenue, New York, New York, with the required registration fee. In a few weeks you will receive a Certificate of Registration with your dog's name (if it is approved) and registration number.

To register with the Field Dog Stud Book, you'll need three forms. Both the owners of your dog's mother and father fill out certificates (if the litter has not already been registered with the F.D.S.B.). Then you fill out the Application for Registration and mail it to the American Field Publishing Company, 222 West Adams Street, Chicago, Illinois, with the fee, and you'll receive your Certificate of Registration.

Actually, all this isn't as complicated as it may appear. It's routine with the dog seller, and the forms are no more complicated than applications for a marriage license or a personal loan.

WORMING AND INOCULATION

Before you take your puppy home, find out from the breeder if he has already been wormed or inoculated for distemper and rabies. Practically all puppies will have worms which they acquire from eating worm eggs, from fleas, or from their mother. The breeder usually gives the puppies a worming before he sells them. If yours has already been wormed, find out when and what treatment was given. The breeder may be able to advise you on any further treatment that is necessary. While there are many commercial worming preparations on the market, it's generally safer to let the vet handle it. There will be more about worms in Chapter 4.

If your puppy has been inoculated against distemper, you will also have to know when this was done so you can give the information to your vet. He will complete the series of shots. If your puppy has not yet been given this protection, your vet should take care of it immediately. Distemper is highly prevalent and contagious. Don't let your puppy out of doors until he has had his distemper shots and they have had time to take effect.

As a rule, kennels and breeders do not inoculate puppies against rabies. In some areas, rabies inoculation is required by law. However, the possibility of your dog becoming affected with rabies, a contact disease, is very slight in most parts of the country. To be perfectly safe, check with your vet who will be familiar with the local ordinances and will advise you.

While the distemper inoculation is permanent and can be supplemented by "booster" shots, rabies inoculation must be repeated yearly. When your puppy receives it, the vet will give you a tag for the dog's collar certifying that he has received the protection. He will also give you a certificate for your own records. For foreign travel and some interstate travel, rabies inoculation is required.

Children and Bassets are a wonderful combination. The Basset is placid and even-tempered and responds to affection and gentle play.

3. Raising the Basset Puppy

Puppies that are old enough to be sold have usually been weaned and can eat solid foods and adapt themselves to life with humans.

The prospect of raising, housebreaking and training a puppy is probably far more frightening than the actual doing. After the first night or two, the pup will become accustomed to his new surroundings and the people who have replaced his littermates as companions. A puppy sleeps most of the time, and with a little attention during his waking hours he will soon become an acceptable family member.

Because of his long body, you must take special care in handling the young Basset. Try not to handle the puppy more than necessary, and when you do have to lift him up, use two hands. Place one hand under his chest to give support and the other under the hindquarters. Be especially careful that you don't drop him and don't let him get anyplace where he will have a long jump to the floor.

Before you bring your puppy home, have a place for him to live. For the first few weeks, he should be confined to one limited area. This will help him orient himself to his new surroundings and will make the business of housebreaking much easier.

HIS LIVING QUARTERS

The average Basset makes a career of spending time in bed and this trait is evident even in the puppy. Prepare a bed for him in a carton or in a draft-free corner of the bedroom or kitchen. Spread out an old blanket, or you can buy cedar shavings at the pet shop and make a comfortable "nest." This also has the advantage of absorbing doggy smells and discouraging fleas. The puppy shouldn't be able to wander from his sleeping quarters until he is reasonably well housebroken—which should take several weeks—so set up some sort of barricade of plywood or heavy cardboard that he cannot climb over.

For the first night or two the puppy probably won't sleep—and neither will you. If he whines and howls, go over to him and give him some companionship. If he persists, try putting a hot water bottle, wrapped in a towel,

This is a typical Basset pose. Give your dog a corner of his own, a comfortable bed, and he'll be perfectly content. But don't forget that he needs exercise too.

next to him. He may snuggle up to it and go to sleep. Sometimes the ticking of a loud alarm clock nearby will be soothing. Above all, don't break down and take the puppy into bed with you, or go to the other extreme and browbeat him into silence. Sleeplessness should pass within a few nights as the puppy becomes more accustomed to his new home.

FEEDING THE PUPPY

A placid dog like the Basset requires less food than a high-strung, nervous dog of the same size. Your new puppy should be nicely plump, so don't worry if he refuses to eat much for the first few days. If the person who sold you the puppy told you what he had been fed, it's a good idea to keep him on the same diet for a while. If you don't know, just go to the nearest supermarket. You'll find an ample variety of dog meal on the shelves, with instructions on the sides of the package for feeding puppies. You can't go wrong if you follow them. However, if the puppy you have is under 8 weeks old, stick to pre-cooked baby cereals (Pablum is good) for the next few weeks. At the corner drug store you can buy dog vitamins in liquid or powder form and some cod-liver oil. Give the puppy a teaspoon of each every day, in his food or directly if he'll take it.

As your dog grows older, decrease the number of meals, but try to feed him at regular times every day.

The latest theory on dog feeding is that puppies do not thrive on milk because of the difference in composition between cow's milk and their mother's. However, some puppies do enjoy milk, so try it and see what results you get.

Until your puppy is 2 months old, he should have four meals a day. Then, omit one meal and feed him three times daily until he is 4 months old. From 4 months to 1 year of age, feed him twice a day. The amount at each feeding should be one ounce of food for each three pounds of the dog's weight.

You have a choice of foods to serve your puppy: baby cereal with a hard-boiled egg mashed into it; dog meal (following instructions on the package) with finely chopped beef or horsemeat added; a mixture of cereal, meal and meat. Add milk or a bland broth to the solid food to bring it to the consistency of a thick mush. As the puppy grows older, give him more solids and less liquids. By the time he is 4 months old you can begin to give him cooked green vegetables or carrots from the table. If you wish, you may use prepared baby foods.

14

Avoid overfeeding. As a rule, a Basset will not overeat and if you give the puppy too many meals a day, he'll just spurn the excess. But watch the dog's fat. After about 4 months the baby fat should begin to go and he should start to look more doggy and less puppyish.

SOME CAUTIONS

If the puppy has continued loose bowels or throws up, it may be a sign of the wrong food, so change his menu. If the condition continues, check with your vet. It may be worms or some serious stomach upset.

If the puppy becomes constipated, give him a small dose of mineral oil, or use a baby-size glycerine suppository.

From the start, try to get the puppy into the habit of eating his meals when they are served. Do not leave his food dish around for hours. If he doesn't eat within a reasonable time, take the food away and don't bring him any more until his next regular mealtime.

Like other members of the hound family, the Basset pup may be a floor-sniffer, taking anything that smells edible into his mouth. Do not leave chicken bones or splintered meat bones where he can get them, and be careful in your use of insecticides around his eating and sleeping areas.

A well-fed dog is neither too fat nor too thin. His coat is sleek, his eyes shiny and his expression alert.

Puppies enjoy playing just as much as children, but the Basset pup's long body is delicate and he should be handled with care.

HOUSEBREAKING THE PUPPY

Housebreaking the puppy isn't difficult because his natural instinct is to keep the place where he sleeps and plays clean. The most important factor is to keep him confined to a fairly small area during the training period. You will find it almost impossible to housebreak a puppy who is given free run of the house. After months of yelling and screaming, you may finally get it through his head that the parlor rug is "verboten," but it will be a long, arduous process.

FIRST, PAPER TRAINING

Spread papers over the puppy's living area. Then watch him carefully. When you notice him starting to whimper, sniff the ground or run around in agitated little circles, rush him to the place that you want to serve as his "toilet" and hold him there till he does his business. Then praise him lavishly. When you remove the soiled papers, leave a small damp piece so that the puppy's sense of smell will lead him back there next time. If he makes a mistake, wash it immediately with warm water, followed by a rinse with water and vinegar. That will kill the odor and prevent discoloration.

It shouldn't take more than a few days for the puppy to get the idea of using newspaper. When he becomes fairly consistent, reduce the area of paper to a few sheets in a corner. As soon as you think he has the idea fixed in his mind, you can let him roam around the house a bit, but keep an eye on him. It might be best to keep him on leash the first few days so you can rush him back to his paper at any signs of an approaching accident.

The normally healthy puppy will want to relieve himself when he wakes up in the morning, after each feeding and after strenuous exercise. During early puppyhood any excitement, such as the return home of a

With a little encouragement, your Basset will soon learn the purpose of the paper on the floor.

The children in your family can help in the outdoor housebreaking of your dog. He should be taken out when he wakes in the morning, after each feeding and after exciting exercise.

member of the family or the approach of a visitor, may result in floor-wetting, but that phase should pass in a few weeks.

OUTDOOR HOUSEBREAKING

Keep in mind during the housebreaking process that you can't expect too much from your puppy until he is about 5 months old. Before that, his muscles and digestive system just aren't under his control. However, you can begin outdoor training even while you are paper training the puppy. (He should have learned to walk on lead at this point. See page 42.) First thing in the morning, take him outdoors (to the curb if you are in a city) and walk him back and forth in a small area until he relieves himself. He will probably make a puddle and then just walk around uncertain of what is expected of him. You can try standing him over a piece of news-paper which may give him the idea. Some dog trainers use glycerine suppositories at this point for fast action. Praise the dog every time taking him outside brings results and he'll get the idea. After each meal take him to the same spot.

The little girl should be taught *never* to hold a Basset like that. She should support the dog's underside with both hands and pick him up only when absolutely necessary.

Use some training word to help your puppy learn. Pick a word that you won't use for any other command and repeat it while you are walking your dog in his outdoor "business" area. It will be a big help when the dog is older if you have some word of command that he can connect with approval to relieve himself in a strange place. You'll find, when you begin the outdoor training, that the male puppy usually requires a longer walk than the female. Both male and female puppies will squat. It isn't until he's quite a bit older that the male dog will begin to lift his leg.

NIGHTTIME TRAINING

If you hate to give up any sleep, you can train your Basset puppy to go outdoors during the day and use the paper at night for the first few months. After he's older, he'll be able to contain himself all night and wait for his first morning walk. However, if you want to speed up the outdoor training so that you can leave the dog alone in the house with less fear of an accident, attach his leash at night so that he has enough room to move around in his bed but not enough to get any distance away from it. When he has to go, he'll whine loudly enough to attract your attention. Then take him or let him out. You may have to get up once or twice a night for a few weeks but then you can be fairly sure that your puppy will behave indoors — although accidents will happen. Sometimes even a grown dog will suddenly — and for no apparent reason — soil the house, usually the most expensive carpet in it.

Occasionally a puppy that seems to have been housebroken will revert to indiscriminate acts all over the place. If that happens it may be necessary to go back to the beginning and repeat the paper training.

WHEN HE MISBEHAVES

Rubbing a puppy's nose in his dirt or whacking him with a newspaper may make you feel better, but it won't help train the puppy. A dog naturally *wants* to do the right thing for his master. Your job is to show him what you want. If an accident happens, ignore it unless you can catch him immediately and then in a firm tone express your displeasure and take him to the spot he should have used. When he does use the right place, be lavish with praise and petting, but first be sure he has finished. Many a puppy has left a trail of water across a floor because someone interrupted him to tell him how well he was doing.

Until the puppy is 7 or 8 months old, be lenient in correcting housebreaking mistakes. After that age the dog should know better and mistakes may be deliberate. Many times an older puppy may soil the house in resentment at being left alone or not getting his way.

Never tie him up or leave his leash on when he's alone in the house. Many puppies have strangled themselves or injured their legs by getting twisted in the leash. This applies to leaving your dog in a car too.

PUPPY DISCIPLINE

A 6- or 8-week-old puppy is old enough to understand what is probably the most important word in his vocabulary—"NO!" The first time you see the puppy doing something he shouldn't do, chewing something he shouldn't chew or wandering in a forbidden area, it's time to teach him. Shout "No" and stamp your foot, hit the table with a piece of newspaper or make some other loud noise. Dogs, especially very young ones, don't like loud noises and your misbehaving pet will readily connect the word with something unpleasant. If he persists, repeat the "No," hold him firmly and slap him sharply across the nose. Before you protest to the A.S.P.C.A. you should realize that a dog does not resent being disciplined if he is doing something wrong and is caught in the act. However, do not chase a puppy around while waving a rolled-up newspaper at him or trying to swat him. Punish him only when you have a firm hold on him. Above all, never call him to you and then punish him. He must learn to associate coming to you with something pleasant.

Every puppy will pick things up. So the second command should be "Drop it!" or "Let go!" Don't engage in a tug-of-war with the puppy, but take the forbidden object from him even if you have to pry his jaws open with your fingers. Many dogs will release what they are holding if you just blow sharply into their faces. Let your dog know that you are displeased when he picks up something he shouldn't.

The Basset isn't usually a furniture-climber, but if you find yours out of bounds, firmly let him know it's not allowed. If your puppy gets on a high piece of furniture, lift him down. Don't let him do any jumping until his legs are developed.

Give your dog something of his own to chew and play with, so he won't be tempted to take a forbidden object.

If you give him toys of his own, he will be less liable to chew your possessions. Avoid soft rubber toys that he can chew to pieces. A firm rubber ball or a tennis ball or a strong piece of leather is a good plaything. Don't give him cloth toys, as he'll probably swallow pieces and have trouble getting them out of his system. Skip the temptation to give him an old slipper, because it will be hard for him to distinguish between that and a brand-new pair you certainly won't want him to chew.

THE NOISY PUPPY

If your Basset is to be kept inside an apartment or alone in a house for long periods, you should start an anti-noise campaign early in puppyhood. Curbing a dog's natural instinct to complain when he's left alone is most easily accomplished when he's young. You'll soon learn the difference between the sound the dog makes when he has to go out or wants food or water and the angry, complaining sound that means temper. Use the loud "No" to show him that you won't tolerate noise. Take hold of his muzzle with both hands and tell him to be quiet.

Use psychology on the dog that howls when he is left alone. Walk out of the room and close the door loudly. Then wait until you hear him making noises. When you do, pound on the door with your hand and command him to keep quiet. Walk back into the room and make sure he stops. Try this a few times. When he finds that noises from him lead to door-pounding and then severe correction from you, he'll quiet down.

However, if you want to have your Basset act as a watchdog, you'll have to use the opposite approach. When he makes his first puppy growls at a footstep outside or at the approach of a stranger, praise and encourage him.

THE FEMALE PUPPY

If you want to spay your female you can have it done while she is still a puppy. Her first seasonal period will probably occur between eight and ten months, although it may be as early as six or delayed until she is a year old. She may be spayed before or after this, or you may breed her (at a later season) and still spay her afterward.

The first sign of the female's being in season is a thin red discharge, which will increase for about a week, when it changes color to a thin yellowish stain, lasting about another week. Simultaneously there is a swelling of the vulva, the dog's external sexual organ. The second week is the crucial period, when she could be bred if you wanted her to have puppies, but it is possible for the period to be shorter or longer, so it is best not to take unnecessary risks at any time. After a third week the swelling decreases and the period is over for about six months.

If you have an absolutely climb-proof and dig-proof run within your yard, it will be safe to leave her there, but otherwise the female in season should be shut indoors. Don't leave her out alone for even a minute; she should be exercised only on leash. If you want to prevent the neighborhood dogs from hanging around your doorstep, as they inevitably will as soon as they discover that your female is in season, take her some distance away from the house before you let her relieve herself. Take her to a nearby park or field in the car for a chance to stretch her legs. After the three weeks are up you can let her out as before, with no worry that she can have puppies until the next season. But if you want to have her spayed, consult your veterinarian about the time and age at which he prefers to do it. With a young dog the operation is simple and after a night or two at the animal hospital she can be at home, wearing only a small bandage as a souvenir.

4. Caring for Your Basset

When he passes his first birthday, your dog can be considered an adult. If you continue the common-sense care you used since he was a puppy, he will enjoy a long, happy and healthy life.

DIET

An adult dog gets along best on one meal a day. You will probably find it most convenient to make this the evening meal and feed your dog at your own dinnertime. However, if you prefer, you can choose another time of the day, but it's best to have a regular schedule and feed your dog at about the same time every day.

The amount of food you give him depends on his activity. Common sense is your best guide. If he rejects certain kinds of foods, don't try to force him to eat them. If you find that some foods upset his stomach, cut them out. The amount of flesh and fat on your dog's body is an indication of his diet's suitability.

Your dog needs fat in his diet. If you are feeding him horsemeat or kibbled or other dry dog foods, add a handful of beef fat or some bacon drippings. Lack of fat will result in a poor coat or dull hair. The adult dog can still use the vitamins or cod-liver oil that you fed the puppy.

If your dog skips an occasional meal, it is no cause for worry. If he isn't interested in eating, take the food away after 10 or 15 minutes. A number of kennels purposely eliminate one meal a week, feeling that it makes the dogs more active and alert. Many exhibitors do not feed their dogs the day of a show. Use your own judgment about that.

Whatever you do, don't pamper your dog as so many pet owners do. Remember that he has a stronger digestive system than you. His internal organs are like those of the fox and the wolf, and under natural conditions he would be eating raw meat without added vitamins or flavoring.

While he can eat almost everything you can, there are some foods you should avoid. A chicken or fish bone can lodge in his throat or cause intestinal trouble. Too many starches or too much sugar in his diet can affect his coat or upset his system since they are not natural foods for

If you have more than one Basset, make sure they all get a chance to eat. This sad-eyed fellow is being kept away from dinner by his more aggressive brothers.

carnivorous animals. However, a piece of candy once in a while, a dish of ice cream or the leavings of a piece of pie won't harm him. When you're traveling, he can enjoy a hamburger or a hot dog as much as the other members of the family.

If your dog develops loose bowels but seems well otherwise, you can try a change of diet. If his meat has been served raw, try cooking it for a few days. Cottage cheese added to the diet often helps, as does barley or oatmeal water instead of plain tap water.

GROOMING THE BASSET

Unlike some of the more finicky breeds, your Basset can get along very well with a minimum of attention from you. Having been bred for many generations as a hunting dog, the Basset's coat is heavy and almost waterproof. He gets dirty, dries out, gives a few shakes and a lick or two and he's clean again! However, from puppyhood on you should accustom him to being handled. It will make trips to the vet much easier and, if you plan to show him, will prepare him for the judge's inspection.

Teach him to jump up on a low platform or bench for his grooming. While he will probably keep himself clean for the most part, you will have a really sleek-looking dog if you allow 10 or 15 minutes a day for a grooming session. At your pet shop or kennel purchase a grooming brush with fairly

Grooming will be easier for you and your dog if you teach him to stand on a platform or bench.

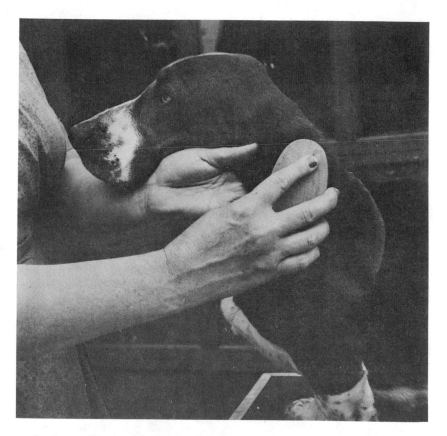

Brush your Basset regularly with a stiff-bristled brush, and don't forget his long, silky ears, but be gentle.

stiff bristles. When you brush your dog, brush down toward his back, and do it vigorously. The purpose of the brushing is not just to improve his appearance but to remove dirt from the hairs and skin and any dead hairs. At the same time you may brush away flea eggs and other parasites. During the summer months examine him carefully for any ticks that may be adhering to his skin. If you find ticks, you must be sure to remove the entire insects. You can touch them with a drop of iodine or a lighted cigarette (be careful not to burn the dog) to break their grip. Then lift them off, one at a time, with a pair of tweezers or a tissue and burn them or drop them into kerosene or gasoline to kill them.

BATHING YOUR DOG

Many Bassets that look and smell very clean have never had a bath. Unless your dog gets into something that just must be washed out of his coat, there is little reason to bathe him. The Saturday night bath is an institution that was never meant to apply to the dog. Frequent bathing will ruin his coat and dry out his skin. If you do feel the need to bathe your dog, use one of the dog soaps with a high oil content. Wash toward the tail so any parasites may be removed. As a precaution, put some cotton into his ears and a few drops of castor oil into his eyes before bathing, to protect them from soap. Rinse him thoroughly with clear water to remove all traces of soap and dry him very carefully. Wrap him in an old towel or use an electric hair dryer and — especially in winter — keep him indoors and out of drafts until he is thoroughly dry.

There are several dry baths on the market, some in aerosol spray cans, that will do a good cleaning job on your dog and will deter or kill fleas or other parasites. You might want to check with your vet before using any of these, as some dogs may develop an allergic reaction to certain chemicals.

CHECK THE EARS AND TEETH

When the Basset eats, his long ears often drop into his food. Make a practice of wiping the ends of his ears after every meal. You may try using a rather high, small-topped feeding dish (many pet shops call them Cocker feeding dishes) to keep his ears out of his food.

NYLABONE® is a necessity that is available at your local petshop (not in supermarkets). The puppy or grown dog chews the hambone flavored nylon into a frilly dog toothbrush, massaging his gums and cleaning his teeth as he plays. Veterinarians highly recommend this product . . . but beware of cheap imitations which might splinter or break.

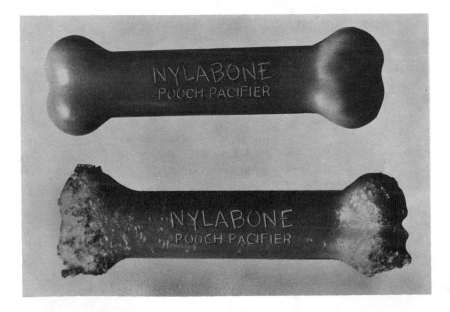

Rinse all the soap from his coat and dry him thoroughly after the bath.

If you see your dog scratching his ears or shaking his head, probe his ears very cautiously with a cotton swab dipped in mineral or castor oil. You may find an accumulation of wax that will work itself out. Any sign of dirt or dried blood in the ears probably indicates ear mites or an infection and requires treatment by your vet. In the summer, especially when flies are heavy, the dog may have sore ears from fly bites. If that happens, wash his ears with warm water and a mild soap, cover with a mild ointment and try to keep him indoors until his ears have healed.

If you give your pet Basset a hard chewing bone — the kind you can buy at a pet store — it will serve him as your tooth brush serves you and will prevent the accumulation of tartar on his teeth. However, check his mouth occasionally and take him to the vet if you find collected tartar or bloody spots on his gums.

WATCH THE TOENAILS

Many dogs that run on gravel or pavements keep their toenails down and seldom need clipping. But a dog that doesn't do much running, or runs on grass, will grow long toenails that can be harmful. The Basset naturally has rather tough toenails, and, especially if he is a house dog, they will grow much faster than they wear down. Overlong nails will force the dog's toes into the air and spread his feet wide. In addition, the nails may force the dog into an unnatural stance that may produce lameness. With proper grooming, the nails should barely touch the floor.

If you are going to clip your dog's toenails, have your vet show you how to do it so you don't cut into the blood vessels.

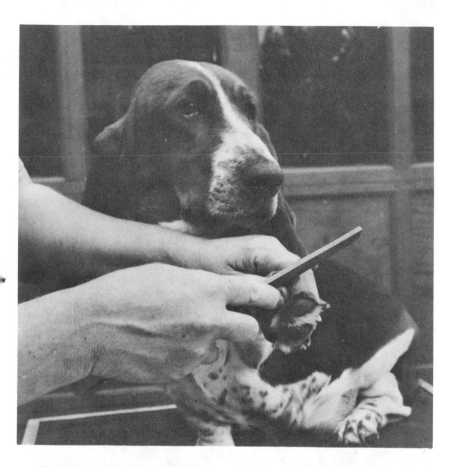

(Above) Many dogs prefer to have their nails filed down rather than clipped. (Below) Your Basset's beauty tools should include a metal comb, brush, scissors, clippers, tooth scraper, file and swabs. A bottle of eye lotion will be useful if his eyes run a bit.

You can control your dog's toenails by cutting them with a special dog clipper or by filing them. Many dogs object to the clipping and it takes some experience to learn just how to do it without cutting into the blood vessels. Your vet will probably examine your dog's nails whenever you bring him in and will trim them at no extra charge. He can show you how to do it yourself in the future. If you prefer, you can file the points off your dog's nails every few weeks with a flat wooden file.

CANINE DISEASES

The Basset is a born "sniffer." He lives in a world in which scent is probably more important than sight and you cannot curb his tendency to travel through life with his nose to the ground. Unfortunately, many dog ailments are spread by germs and viruses which your Basset can pick up through his nose. No matter how proud you are of your pet, keep him in-

Haircut? No, just trimming some of the coarse hairs off the Basset's muzzle to give him a more gentlemanly—or is it ladylike?—appearance. Use a blunt pair of scissors, and make sure he holds still.

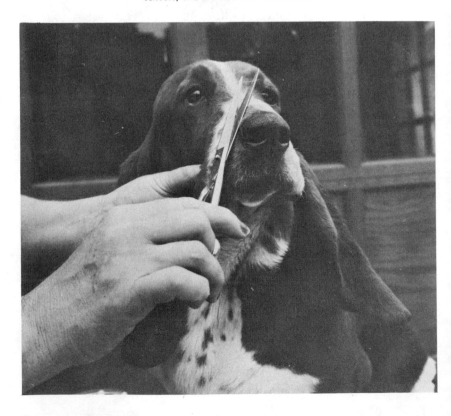

Just a short grooming session daily will give you a sleek, well-tended dog.

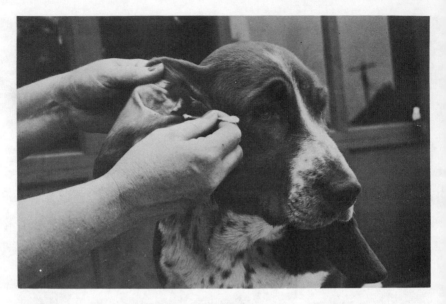

To clean your dog's ears, use a swab dipped in mineral or castor oil. Don't probe too deeply. If there is any sign of ear mites or infection, get your vet's advice.

doors until he has had his protective permanent distemper shots and other inoculations your veterinarian may recommend.

With early inoculations, a proper diet, enough exercise and human companionship, your dog should continue to remain healthy. However, you should be familiar with the more common diseases that may affect dogs and with the symptoms that may help you to recognize them in time to get your dog to a veterinarian for prompt treatment.

Rabies: This is an acute disease of the dog's central nervous system and is spread by the bite of an infected animal, the saliva carrying the infection. Rabies occurs in two forms. The first is "Furious Rabies" in which the dog shows a period of melancholy or depression, then irritation, and finally paralysis. The first period lasts from a few hours to several days. During this time, the dog is cross and will try to hide from members of the family. He appears restless and will change his position often. He loses his appetite for food and begins to lick, bite and swallow foreign objects. During the "irritation" phase the dog is spasmodically wild and has impulses to run away. He acts in a fearless manner and runs and bites at everything in sight. If he is caged or confined he will fight at the bars, often breaking teeth or fracturing his jaw. His bark becomes a peculiar howl. In the final or paralysis stage, the animal's lower jaw becomes paralyzed and hangs down; he walks with a stagger and saliva drips from his mouth. Within four to eight days after the onset of paralysis, the dog dies.

The second form of rabies, "Dumb Rabies," is characterized by the dog's walking in a bear-like manner with his head down. The lower jaw is paralyzed and the dog is unable to bite. Outwardly it may seem as though he has a bone caught in his throat.

Even if your pet should be bitten by a rabid dog or other animal, he can probably be saved if you get him to the vet in time for a series of injections. However, by the time the symptoms appear the disease is so far advanced that no cure is possible. But remember that an annual rabies inoculation is almost certain protection against rabies.

Distemper: Young dogs are most susceptible to distemper, although it may affect dogs of all ages. The dog will lose his appetite, seem depressed, chilled, and run a fever. Often he will have a watery discharge from his eyes and nose. Unless treated promptly, the disease goes into advanced stages with infections of the lungs, intestines and nervous system, and dogs that recover

This isn't as painful as it appears. With a tooth scraper, it's easy to remove light tartar deposits from your Basset's teeth to keep his gums healthy. Heavy deposits require professional treatment.

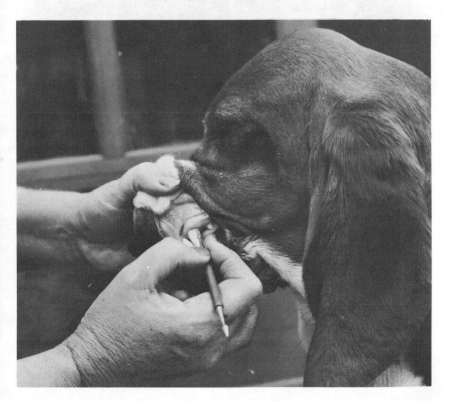

With the necessary inoculations and common-sense care, your pet will stay healthy and happy.

may be left with some impairment such as a twitch or other nervous mannerism. The best protection against this is very early inoculation — preferably even before the puppy is old enough to go out into the street and meet other dogs.

Hepatitis: Veterinarians report an increase in the spread of this virus disease in recent years, usually with younger dogs as the victims. The initial symptoms — drowsiness, vomiting, great thirst, loss of appetite and a high temperature — closely resemble distemper. These symptoms are often accompanied by swellings on the head, neck and lower parts of the belly. The disease strikes quickly and death may occur in a few hours. Protection is afforded by injection with a new vaccine.

Leptospirosis: This disease is caused by bacteria which live in stagnant or slow-moving water. It is carried by rats and dogs, and many dogs are believed to get it from licking the urine or feces of infected rats. The symptoms are increased thirst, depression and weakness. In the acute stage, there is vomiting, diarrhea and a brown discoloration of the jaws, tongue and teeth, caused by an inflammation of the kidneys. This disease can be cured if caught in time, but it is best to ward it off with a vaccine which your vet can administer along with the distemper shots.

Skin Ailments: Any skin diseases that affect your Basset require professional treatment. Some are transmittable to humans; others take a long time to cure. Small, bare, scaly spots around the eyes may indicate the presence of red mange. Examine the skin on the flanks or legs for pimply blotches with an unpleasant odor. This is the result of another type of mange. Your vet can provide you with medicine and treatment is usually successful, although a deep-seated infection may require a fairly long course of treatment.

Stuffed Anal Glands: The dog has two glands which open into his rectum. Sometimes these glands become stuffed and cause much discomfort to

Bassets need fresh air, sunshine and play as much as your children do.

the animal. If your dog rubs his rear end to the ground or on furniture, constantly licks at it, and if you can see or feel a swelling in the rectal area, that's probably the trouble. The remedy is to squeeze the matter out of the glands, which you can usually do yourself, using absorbent cotton and squeezing in and upward. If left alone, the glands will abcess and open. A serious case should be lanced by the vet.

Constipation or Diarrhea: Normally an adult dog should have two bowel movements a day, although some have one, some three. If your dog is constipated, give him a dose of milk of magnesia or mineral oil (for a grown dog, use the same amount prescribed for an adult human; for a puppy, a baby dose). You might also add some liver to his diet. Never use human laxatives on your dog. If the condition persists, see the vet.

Diarrhea can be caused by a change in diet or drinking water, excitement, worms or other things. Infrequent diarrhea can be ignored, but if it persists, cut down on the amount of drinking water and substitute oatmeal or barley water. A meal of cottage cheese has been found effective in many cases. Again, if that doesn't help, see the vet, especially if there are other symptoms of illness at the same time.

Worms: There are six different types of worms that can affect puppies and grown dogs. If your puppy has been properly wormed, he may go through life without ever needing the treatment again. However, dogs that are allowed to run loose or those that pick up fleas will usually develop worms. As to treatment, there are a number of patent medicines on the market, but a trip to the vet is usually a better idea than a do-it-yourself cure. Some types of worms can be detected only by microscopic examination of the stool.

Running Eyes: Because of the characteristic folds of skin around his eyes, your Basset's eyes may run sometimes. If this happens, wash out his eyes daily with a mild boric acid solution or other eye wash recommended by your vet.

Coughs and Colds: Your dog is almost as liable to come down with a cough or cold as you are, but the human and canine types are different and can't be transmitted to each other. Treat the dog's cold much as you would your own. Keep him quieter than usual, give him aspirin, and put him on a light diet. Don't try to train or work him while he's coughing or sneezing. If your dog's sleeping quarters are out of drafts and in a fairly warm place, colds will be kept to a minimum.

THE USEFUL THERMOMETER

Almost every serious puppy ailment shows itself by an increase in the puppy's body temperature. If your dog seems to act lifeless, looks dull-eyed and gives an impression of illness, check by using a rectal thermometer. Hold the dog, insert the thermometer which has been lubricated with vaseline and take a reading. The normal temperature is 100.6 to 101.5 (higher than the normal human temperature). Excitement may send it up slightly, but any rise of more than a few points is cause for alarm.

FIRST AID FOR YOUR DOG

In general, a dog will lick his cuts and wounds and they'll heal. If he swallows anything harmful, chances are he'll throw it up. But it will probably make you feel better to help him if he's hurt, so treat his wounds as you would your own. Wash out the dirt and apply an antiseptic or ointment. If you put on a bandage, you'll have to do something to keep the dog from trying to remove it. A large cardboard ruff around his neck will prevent him from licking his chest or body. You can tape up his nails to keep him from scratching, or make a "bootie" for his paws.

If you think your dog has a broken bone, before moving him apply a splint just as you would to a person's limb. If there is bleeding that won't stop, apply a tourniquet between the wound and heart, but loosen it every few minutes to prevent damage to the circulatory system.

If you are afraid that your dog has swallowed poison and you can't get the vet fast enough, try to induce vomiting by giving him a strong solution of salt water or mustard in water.

SOME "BUTS"

First, don't be frightened by the number of diseases a dog can get. The majority of dogs never get any of them. If you need assurance, look at any book on human diseases. How many have you had?

Don't become a dog-hypochondriac. Veterinarians have enough work taking care of sick dogs and doing preventive work with their patients. Don't rush your pet to the vet every time he sneezes or seems tired. All dogs have days on which they feel lazy and want to lie around doing nothing.

Your dog will stay healthy if he has a proper diet, enough exercise to keep him from getting fat and lazy and something—such as obedience or field training—to keep his mind occupied and give him an interest in life.

5. Training Your Basset

When you train your Basset, you have to adjust yourself to his slow, somewhat plodding type of personality. However, don't make the mistake of thinking that because he is slow-moving he is not smart. You can't put over what Madison Avenue calls a "fast sell" on a Basset. During training sessions, give him time to think over each lesson and work at his own pace. Bassets hate to be forced to do anything, so try to make the lessons as much of a game as possible. If you show enthusiasm every time he does something correctly, you'll find him responding to you and working with you.

PURPOSE OF TRAINING

The purpose of training is, first, to prepare your family pet to take his place in society and to become an acceptable member of the community. In the dog-person relationship, the person gives the orders and the dog should be taught to obey willingly. For his own safety the dog must be taught to stop when he is told to stop, to keep out of the road, to keep away from people's possessions.

HOW A DOG LEARNS

The dog is the one domestic animal that seems to want to do what his master asks. Unlike other animals that learn by fear or rewards, the dog will work willingly if he is given a kind word or a show of affection.

The hardest part of dog training is communication. If you can get across to the dog what you want him to do, he'll do it. Always remember that your dog does not understand the English language. He can, however, interpret your tone of voice and your gestures. By associating certain words with the act that accompanies them, the dog can acquire a fairly large working vocabulary. Keep in mind that it is the sound rather than the meaning of the words that the dog understands.

YOUR PART IN TRAINING

You must patiently demonstrate to your dog what each simple word of command means. Guide him with your hands and the training leash through whatever routine you are teaching him. Repeat the word associated with the act. Demonstrate again and again to give the dog the chance to make the connection in his mind. (In psychological language, you are conditioning him to give a specific response to a specific stimulus.)

Once he begins to get the idea, use the word of command without any physical guidance. Drill him. When he makes mistakes, correct him, kindly at first, more severely as his training progresses.

When he does what you want, praise him lavishly with words and with pats. Don't rely on dog candy or treats in training. The dog that gets into the habit of performing for treats will seldom be fully dependable when he can't smell or see one in the offing.

THE TRAINING VOICE

When you start to give your dog lessons, use your training voice, giving commands in a firm, loud tone. Once you give the command, persist until it is obeyed even if you have to pull the dog protestingly to obey you.

Your dog wants to please you, and if you are patient and affectionate he will respond well to training.

He must learn that training is different from playing, that a command once given must be obeyed no matter what distractions are present.

Be consistent in the use of words during training. Confine your commands to as few words as possible and never change them. It is best for only one person to carry on the dog's training because different people will use different words and tactics that will confuse the animal. The dog who hears "come," "get over here," "hurry up," "here, Rover" and other commands when he is wanted will become totally confused.

TAKE IT EASY

Training is hard on the dog — and on the trainer. A young dog just cannot take more than 10 minutes of training at a stretch, so limit the length of your first lessons. You'll find that you, too, will tend to become impatient when you stretch out a training session, and losing your temper won't help either of you. Before and after each lesson have a play period, but don't play during a training session. Even the youngest dog soon learns that schooling is a serious matter; fun comes afterward.

Don't spend too much time on one phase of training or the dog will become bored. And always try to end a training session on a pleasant note. If the dog doesn't seem to be getting what you are trying to show him, go back to something simpler that he can do. This way you will end every lesson with a pleasant feeling of accomplishment. Actually, in nine cases out of ten, if your dog isn't doing what you want, it's because you're not getting the idea over to him properly.

Your very young puppy should have learned to keep away from things that didn't belong to him and to be quiet when alone, discussed in Chapter 3. Now that he's a little older, you are ready for his further training.

WALKING ON LEAD

"Doggy" people call the leash a "lead," so we'll use that term here. Fortunately, the great majority of Bassets take to the lead very easily. The best lead for training purposes is the 6-foot webbed-cloth lead, usually olive-drab in color.

As for the collar, you'll need a metal-link collar called a "choke" collar. Even though the name may sound frightening, it won't hurt your dog and it's an absolute *must* in training. It tightens when you snap the lead, eases when you relax your grip. Trying to train a young dog with an ordinary leather collar is almost impossible. You'll probably have to get two or three collars in progressively larger sizes as your dog grows larger, so don't spend too much on the first one you buy. It's important to put the collar on properly. Slide the chain around your dog's neck so that you can attach the lead to the ring at the end of the chain which passes *over*, not under his neck.

With your dog on your left, hold the lead firmly in your right hand. Use your left hand to jerk the lead when corrections are necessary.

Put the collar and lead on the puppy and let him walk around the house first with the lead dragging on the floor. This is just to let him get the feel of the strange object around his neck. But a word of caution for afterward: don't let the dog wander around with the choke collar on. If it's loose he'll lose it, and it's possible for it to catch on any projection and choke him. For his license tag and rabies tag you can get a light leather collar that fits more snugly.

Now, here's a lesson for you. From the start, hold the lead firmly in your right hand. Keep the dog at your left side. You can use your left hand to jerk the lead when necessary to give corrections or to bring the dog closer to you. Do not *pull* on the lead. Give it a sharp snap when you want to correct the dog, and then release it. The dog cannot learn from being pulled around. He will learn when he finds that doing certain things results in a sharp jerk; doing other things allows him to walk comfortably on lead.

At first, the puppy will fight the lead. He'll probably plant all four feet or his rear end on the ground and wait for your next move. Be patient. Short tugs on the lead will help him learn his part in walking with you. If he

In a short time, your Basset will be walking comfortably on lead, adjusting his pace to yours.

gets overexcited, calm him before taking off the lead and collar and picking him up. He must learn there's nothing to fear. (Incidentally, if the lesson is being given on a city street, it might be a good idea to carry some paper to clean up the mess he may leave in his excitement.)

TEACHING THE "SIT" AND "DOWN"

Teaching the Basset to sit on command presents no problems. You'll find that whenever he stops he'll either sit or flop down. To teach him to sit on command hold his chest with one hand, press down firmly on his hindquarters with the other and repeat the word "Sit." Do not let him lie down or stand up. After he has been sitting for a moment say "Okay" and praise him. Always wait a short time after he sits before praising him so he knows he has to remain sitting for a while. After one or two demonstrations, he should sit at the command, and you won't have to push him down. If he's on lead, you can pull up on it slightly as you push his rear end down and keep him in a sitting position until you relax the pressure on his collar.

It might seem that a dog that spends so much time lying on the floor or in his bed would lie down on command with no trouble. But you must remember that the words "lie down" have no meaning to the dog until you have associated them with the act you demand from him. For this it's best to have him on lead. First sit him, and stand in front of him. Run the lead under your left shoe. As you give the command "Down," pull on the lead. That will pull the dog's head down. At the same time, lean forward and push his hindquarters down to the floor. There may be a bit of a struggle, but as soon as you have him firmly down for a moment tell him what a good dog he is, release him, and start all over.

If you have trouble getting your dog down from the front, stay at his

Training is a serious business and this Basset looks as if he realizes it as he concentrates on his sit-and-stay lesson.

When you teach your Basset to lie down, slide the lead under your left foot and pull on it. Then use the "stay" signal with your left hand to keep him down.

side, keeping him to your left. Pull his front legs out from under him as you say the word "Down." Teaching this may be the first contest of wills between you and your dog. The average dog will sit without any fuss, but many resent being told they have to lie down. However, if you're persistent your dog will give in.

After a while your dog will lie down on command alone or on command with the aid of a downward tug on the lead. At that stage you can begin to teach him the hand signal. Whenever you use the command "Down," raise your right hand, palm down, at about shoulder level. That's the universal hand signal to lie down, and soon the dog will associate it with the command and will drop on either the voice signal or the hand signal.

MORE ADVANCED TRAINING

The puppy that has learned to walk on lead, sit and lie down on command is ready for advanced training. However, don't start this until your Basset is about 6 months old, unless he happens to be very precocious.

Whether your dog is to be a house pet, a hunter or a show dog, he will benefit from some obedience training. The basis of all further training is "heeling," training the dog to walk at your left knee, adjusting his pace to yours, whether he is on lead or off. If you try a few heeling lessons and get no response, it may indicate that the dog just isn't mature enough for training yet, so wait another month or so.

TEACHING YOUR DOG TO HEEL

Any walk with your dog can become a heeling lesson. Sit the dog, on lead, at your left side and then start off at a brisk pace. As you start, use the dog's name and the command "Heel!" and tug sharply at the lead. Always start walking with your left foot. After a while your dog will learn to watch that foot for a clue to whether to start, stop or turn with you.

If the dog forges ahead or drops back, snap him into position with a jerk on the lead, but work with a fairly long lead so that you are directing him by snapping and relaxing it rather than pulling him along with you.

Remember that praise is an important part of learning. When your dog does well, let him know that you're pleased.

As soon as you stop walking, your dog should automatically sit in the heel position, at your left knee.

Make the dog understand that this training is a serious business, and don't allow any nonsense. If he tries to sniff the ground, pull his head up and tell him off. If he is distracted by another dog, make a sharp turn in the opposite direction and give the lead a good yank. You won't hurt your dog by a little firmness at this time.

During the first few heeling lessons, every time you halt tell the dog to sit or push his hindquarters down. Soon he'll sit automatically whenever you stop. Don't let him develop a "sloppy" sit. He should sit right at your left knee, facing forward in the same direction you are facing, about six inches from your leg. The length of his body sometimes makes it difficult for the Basset to sit properly. While he should sit squarely, he may instead sit in a sort of semicircle with his head in approximately the right position but his rear end behind you. To correct this, don't try to pull him into position, but take another couple of steps forward and try to get him to sit correctly.

As you practice heeling, have a running conversation with your dog to keep his attention focused on you. Whenever you stop and he sits properly, praise him. At first you may feel ridiculous walking around talking to the dog, but you'll soon get into the spirit of it when you see how well he responds.

NEW! This new Material Handling Set is specially designed to create a world of Tonka fun— for under $12.00

Tonka fun lasts and lasts.

Tonka fun lasts through sand and summer.

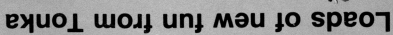

Loads of new fun from Tonka

NEW

NEW! Realistic Regular Tonka Ramp Hoist and Loader. The truck bed tips to make a ramp for true to life loader transport for imaginative construction play.

NEW! Mini Tonka Landscape Truck and Loader. Plenty of play action here. Loader has working scoop and fits on truck trailer for long hauls to the job.

NEW

NEW

NEW! Mini Tonka Sanitary Truck — Bright green and white truck really works to clean up after the roadwork's been done.

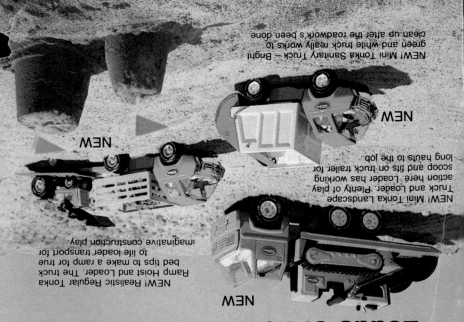

Time-tested play value classics

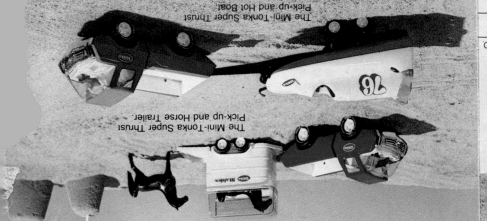

The Mini-Tonka Super Thrust Pick-up and Horse Trailer.

The Mini-Tonka Super Thrust Pick-up and Hot Boat.

Tonka fun lasts and lasts.

Tonka Fun Lasts and Lasts.

Single toys, two toys in one, or toys in sets, Tonka Toys are designed to offer your children endless play value. And there's a Tonka Toy priced to fit every family's budget. Your children can come back and play with their Tonka Toys day after day . . . Because we at Tonka are parents too, every Tonka Toy is safe, tough and built to last through sand, summer and childhood.

There's no end to the fun with Tonka Toys.

POWERED . . . SPEEDY . . . TOUGH

Tonka Toy, the fun lasts and lasts!
Dragsters! They're fast, fun, and like any
Motor bikes! Speedy Scramblers! Racing
let go . . . and they're off. Action Race Cars!
Press down . . . move ahead . . .

SPRING POWERED

Action

TONKA ACTION TOYS
DO NOT USE BATTERIES

To make the heeling lessons more interesting to your dog, vary the routine. You can start by walking normally, then go into a fast pace, slow down to a very slow walk, break into a slow run. Make right and left turns and about-face. Interrupt your heeling with reviews of sit, down and stay commands.

When your dog will heel along with you on a slack lead and will follow you closely on about-faces and left and right turns, try heeling him off lead. First throw the end of the lead over your shoulder and go through a few minutes of the heeling exercises. If he follows you well, remove the lead from the collar. Use voice commands to keep him near you. If he wanders, lags or forges ahead, or swings too wide on your turns, put the lead back and correct him. If he takes the opportunity to bolt away, count to ten, and then correct him severely.

Do not be too anxious to try off-lead heeling before your dog is letter-perfect at heeling on lead. And don't try to show off by taking your dog on a busy street without a lead until he's well settled and absolutely certain to obey every command.

TEACHING THE "COME"

Wave a piece of food, dog candy or a stick and say "Come," and your pet Basset will come a-running. Getting him to come every time you call him is a different matter. Sit him and walk him to the end of the lead, facing him. Say his name and "Come" in your most coaxing tone of voice (here it's okay to coax). Give the lead a sharp tug. When he comes directly

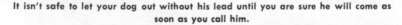

It isn't safe to let your dog out without his lead until you are sure he will come as soon as you call him.

When your Basset comes to you on command, be lavish in your praise.

to you, make a big fuss over him. Repeat this a few times. After he has gotten over the initial excitement of his new learning, make him sit in front of you whenever he comes. As soon as he gets the idea of coming from the end of the lead, tie a longer piece of cord to the lead and have him come a greater distance. Then try it without the lead. Again, do not do this until he is fully trained and comes every time with the lead and cord attached. Once he gets the idea of running away on a "Come" command, you're in for another battle of beast vs. man.

TEACHING TO COME TO HEEL

The object of this is for you to stand still, say "Heel!" and have your dog come right over to you and sit by your left knee in heel position. If your dog has been trained to sit without command every time you stop, he's ready for this step.

Sit him in front of and facing you and step back a few feet. Say "Heel" in your most commanding tone of voice and pull the dog into heel position, making him sit. There are several different ways to do this. You can swing the dog around behind you from your right side, behind your back and to heel position. Or you can pull him toward you, keep him on your left side and swing him to heel position. Use your left heel to straighten him out if he begins to sit behind you or crookedly. This may take a little work, but the dog will get the idea if you show him just what you want.

In this lesson, you must do most of the work. Step forward as you swing your dog into position. Take two or three steps until he is alongside you. When he is in the right spot, pull upward on the lead and either push his back down or slap his rump to get him down. In later practice sessions, sit the dog, take a few steps forward and say "Heel." Step to his right and give the command, then step behind him and repeat it. When he's working well enough on lead, try off lead. At the first sign of sloppiness, get him back on lead for more drilling.

TEACHING THE "STAY"

The next step in training is teaching the dog to stay put in either a sitting or down position. Sit the dog at your left side and put your left

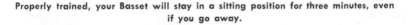

Properly trained, your Basset will stay in a sitting position for three minutes, even if you go away.

Make sure your dog understands exactly what you want of him during training sessions.

hand in front of his nose while ordering him to "Stay!" If he starts to move, push him back to a sit. If he begins to rise, bounce your left hand gently off his nose, all the while repeating the order "Stay!" Do not use his name with this command.

Move slowly around the dog, watching him carefully. If he begins to move, again shove him back into position. When you are facing him, move backward slowly, holding the lead. Be careful not to jerk it. When you are at the end of the lead, drop it. If the dog moves, correct him sharply.

Do not expect too much at first. A short "stay" will show that the dog has the idea. In further lessons you can make him stay for a longer time, until he will sit for three minutes or so without moving.

At the same time as you teach him to stay in a sitting position, you can teach him to stay while down. Keep close to him at first, correcting his verbally and putting him back into position if he should move. Then walk around and step over him while he is down.

After he is responding well to the "stay" command, try telling him to stay and then walking out of sight, at first for a few seconds, later for longer periods. With more training, your dog should sit for three minutes and stay down for five minutes or even longer with you out of the room or hidden from sight.

DOG TRAINING SCHOOLS

The Basset that has been trained to heel, come, sit, lie down and stay has absorbed the basic elements of obedience training. Despite the arguments of some trainers that Bassets can't be trained in obedience work, many have qualified in shows and won obedience certificates from the American Kennel Club.

However, there is a limit to the amount of training you can accomplish when you work alone with your dog. The dog must be able to follow commands and work when there are other dogs around, and the best place for him to learn this is at a dog training school where there are other dogs and their handlers.

There are dog training classes in almost every city. Some are conducted by the local A.S.P.C.A., some by dog training clubs and some by professional trainers. If you turn your dog over to a professional trainer, you will miss a lot of the fun of working with him. However, if you prefer doing it this way, make sure you receive the necessary instructions to carry on the training when the dog is with you.

Despite his short legs, your Basset can jump in and out of cars without help. If he does much traveling to school, shows or field trials, a private roomette will be convenient.

OBEDIENCE TRIALS

The A.K.C. obedience trials are divided into four classes: Novice, Open, Utility and Tracking.

In the Novice Class, the dog will be judged on the following basis:

Test	Maximum Score
Heel on leash	35
Stand for examination by judge	30
Heel free—off leash	45
Recall (come on command)	30
1-minute sit	30
3-minute down	30
Maximum total score	200

If the dog "qualifies" in three different shows by earning at least 50 per cent of the points for each test, with a total of at least 170 for the trial, he has earned the Companion Dog degree and the letters C.D. are entered in the stud book after his name.

After the dog has qualified as a C.D., he is eligible to enter the Open Class competition where he will be judged on this basis:

Test	Maximum Score
Heel free	40
Drop on recall	30
Retrieve (wooden dumbbell) on flat	25
Retrieve over obstacle (hurdle)	35
Broad jump	20
3-minute sit (handler out of sight)	25
5-minute down (handler out of sight)	25
Maximum total score	200

Again he must qualify in three shows for the C.D.X. (Companion Dog Excellent) title and then is eligible for the Utility Class where he can earn the Utility Dog degree in these rugged tests:

Test	Maximum Score
Scent discrimination (picking up article handled by master from group of articles — Article #1	20
Scent discrimination — Article #2	20
Scent discrimination — Article #3	20
Seek back (picking up article dropped by handler)	30
Signal exercise (heeling, etc., on hand signal only)	35
Directed jumping (over hurdle and bar jump)	40
Group examination	35
Maximum total score	200

The dog that earns the coveted U.D. and his handler can both be very proud of the accomplishment.

In the Tracking Test, the dog must follow the trail of a stranger over open country, working at the end of a long lead held by his handler. First, the dog's tracking must be observed and a licensed tracking judge has to approve him as ready for the test. Then he must qualify by completing a tracking test under specified conditions, with three or more dogs competing and two qualified judges observing. Tracking tests are held separately from other obedience tests. The dog that qualifies receives the title T.D.—Tracking Dog. Usually dogs take up tracking after they have earned their U.D. (although this is not required) and then receive the full title of U.D.T. — Utility Dog, Tracker.

For more complete information about obedience trials, write to the American Kennel Club, 221 Fourth Avenue, New York, New York, and ask for their free booklet "Regulations and Standards for Obedience Trials."

FIELD TRIALS

The Basset's natural instincts have readied him to work in the field as a hunter. All he needs is the opportunity and the chance to be shown what to do. If you have hunted with dogs before, you will find the Basset a steady sure scent hound. He'll seldom rely on his eyes in the field, using his nose exclusively. If you're a beginner at hunting with a dog, find someone with experience to set you and your dog on the right track.

Because he has had generations of selective breeding to produce a hunting dog, the Basset may show to better advantage in the field trial than in the obedience ring or breed show. In a field trial the dog performs under actual hunting conditions and is judged on his ability to perform intelligently. Many persons who have known the Basset only as a house pet are amazed at the transformation that takes place when the dog is given the chance to run rabbits in the field. He seems to come alive.

The field trial as far as possible simulates an actual rabbit hunting trip, except that guns aren't used. They are run under a license granted by the A.K.C. The best source of information about these trials is the American Field Magazine, 222 West Adams Street, Chicago 6, Illinois.

Most of the trials are held in the spring and fall in the North, in the winter in the South. When you are traveling, watch for roadside arrows and signs announcing "Field Trial."

The dog in a field trial is judged on his hunting ability, the way he performs in the field under hunting conditions. Entry fees for a field trial range from $1 to $75, and the prizes are in proportion, although the cash awards are secondary to the thrill of winning.

Dogs work in a brace, two dogs together. They are paired by drawing. The judges have a 10-point scale of values by which they judge the dogs in competition. A number of Bassets have earned their field championships.

6. Caring for the Female and Raising Puppies

Whether or not you bought your female dog intending to breed her, some preparation is necessary when and if you decide to take this step.

WHEN TO BREED

It is usually best to breed on the second or third season. Plan in advance the time of year which is best for you, taking into account where the puppies will be born and raised. You will keep them until they are at least six weeks old, and a litter of husky pups takes up considerable space by then. Other considerations are selling the puppies (Christmas vs. springtime sales), your own vacation, and time available to care for them. You'll need at least an hour a day to feed and clean up after the mother and puppies but probably it will take you much longer — with time out to admire and play with them!

CHOOSING THE STUD

You can plan to breed your female about 6½ months after the start of her last season, although a variation of a month or two either way is not unusual. Choose the stud dog and make arrangements well in advance. If you are breeding for show stock, which may command better prices, a mate should be chosen with an eye to complementing the deficiencies of your female. If possible, the dogs should have several ancestors in common within the last two or three generations, as such combinations generally "click" best. The male should have a good show record or be the sire of show winners if old enough to be proven.

The owner of such a male usually charges a fee for the use of the dog. This does not guarantee a litter, but you generally have the right to breed your female again if she does not have puppies. In some cases the owner of the stud will agree to take a choice puppy in place of a stud fee. You should settle all details beforehand, including the possibility of a single surviving puppy, deciding the age at which he is to make his choice and take the pup, and so on.

If you want to raise a litter "just for the fun of it" and plan merely to

If you want the fun of raising a litter of pups, choose your dog's mate on the basis of health and disposition. (By the way, the toenails on these Bassets are far too long and are pushing their toes apart so that their feet look splayed.)

make use of an available male, the most important selection point is temperament. Make sure the dog is friendly as well as healthy, because a bad disposition could appear in his puppies, and this is the worst of all traits in a dog destined to be a pet. In such cases a "stud fee puppy," not necessarily the choice of the litter, is the usual payment.

PREPARATION FOR BREEDING

Before you breed your female, make sure she is in good health. She should be neither too thin nor too fat. Any skin disease *must* be cured before it can be passed on to the puppies. If she has worms she should be wormed before being bred or within three weeks afterward. It is generally considered a good idea to revaccinate her against distemper and hepatitis before the puppies are born. This will increase the immunity the puppies receive during their early, most vulnerable period.

The female will probably be ready to breed 12 days after the first colored discharge. You can usually make arrangements to board her with the owner of the male for a few days, to insure her being there at the proper time, or you can take her to be mated and bring her home the same day. If she still appears receptive she may be bred again two days later. However, some females never show signs of willingness, so it helps to have the experience of a breeder. Usually the second day after the discharge changes color is the proper time, and she may be bred for about three days following. For an additional week or so she may have some discharge and attract other dogs by her odor, but can seldom be bred.

THE FEMALE IN WHELP

You can expect the puppies nine weeks from the day of breeding, although 61 days is as common as 63. During this time the female should receive normal care and exercise. If she was overweight, don't increase her food at first; excess weight at whelping time is bad. If she is on the thin side build her up, giving some milk and biscuit at noon if she likes it. You may add one of the mineral and vitamin supplements to her food to make sure that the puppies will be healthy. As her appetite increases, feed her more. During the last two weeks the puppies grow enormously and she will probably have little room for food and less appetite. She should be tempted with meat, liver and milk, however.

As the female in whelp grows heavier, cut out violent exercise and jumping. Although a dog used to such activities will often play with the children or run around voluntarily, restrain her for her own sake.

PREPARING FOR THE PUPPIES

Prepare a whelping box a few days before the puppies are due, and allow the mother to sleep there overnight or to spend some time in it during the day to become accustomed to it. Then she is less likely to try to have her pups under the front porch or in the middle of your bed. A variety of places will serve, such as a corner of your cellar, garage, or an unused room. If the weather is warm, a large outdoor doghouse will do, well protected from rain or draft. A whelping box serves to separate mother and puppies from visitors and other distractions. The walls should be high enough to restrain the puppies, yet allow the mother to get away from the puppies after she has fed them. Three feet square is minimum size, and six-inch walls will keep the pups in until they begin to climb, when the walls should be built up. Then the puppies really need more room anyway, so double the space with a very low partition down the middle and you will find them naturally housebreaking themselves.

Layers of newspaper spread over the whole area will make excellent bedding and be absorbent enough to keep the surface warm and dry. They should be removed daily and replaced with another thick layer. An old quilt or washable blanket makes better footing for the nursing puppies than slippery newspaper during the first week, and is softer for the mother.

Be prepared for the actual whelping several days in advance. Usually the female will tear up papers, refuse food and generally act restless. These may be false alarms; the real test is her temperature, which will drop to below 100° about 12 hours before whelping. Take it with a rectal thermometer morning and evening, and when the temperature goes down put her in the pen, looking in on her frequently.

WHELPING

Usually little help is needed but it is wise to stay close to make sure that the mother's lack of experience does not cause an unnecessary accident. Be ready to help when the first puppy arrives, for it could smother if the mother does not break the membrane enclosing it. She should start right away to lick the puppy, drying and stimulating it, but you can do it with a soft rough towel instead. The afterbirth should follow the birth of each puppy, attached to the puppy by the long umbilical cord. Watch to make sure that each is expelled, for retaining this material can cause infection. In her instinct for cleanliness the mother will probably eat the afterbirth after biting the cord. One or two will not hurt her; they stimulate milk supply as well as labor for remaining pups. But too many can make her lose appetite for the food she needs to feed her pups and regain her strength. So remove the rest of them along with the wet newspapers and keep the pen dry and clean to relieve her anxiety.

If the mother does not bite the cord, or does it too close to the body, take over the job, to prevent an umbilical hernia. Tearing is recommended, but you can cut it, about two inches from the body, with a sawing motion of scissors that have been sterilized in alcohol. Then dip the end of the cord in a shallow dish of iodine; the cord will dry up and fall off in a few days.

The puppies should follow each other at intervals of not more than half an hour. If more time goes past and you are sure there are still pups to come, a brisk walk outside may start labor again. If your dog is actively straining without producing a puppy it may be presented backward, a so-called "breech" or upside-down birth. Careful assistance with a well-soaped finger to feel for the puppy or ease it back may help, but never attempt to pull it by force against the mother. This could cause serious damage, so let an expert handle it.

If anything seems wrong, waste no time in calling your veterinarian who can examine her and if necessary give hormones which will bring the remaining puppies. You may want his experience in whelping the litter even if all goes well. He will probably prefer to have the puppies born at his hospital rather than to get up in the middle of the night to come to your home. The mother would, no doubt, prefer to stay at home, but you can be sure she will get the best of care in his hospital.

RAISING THE PUPPIES

Hold each puppy to a breast as soon as he is dry, for a good meal without competition. Then he may join his littermates in a basket out of his mother's way while she is whelping. Keep a supply of evaporated milk on hand for emergencies, or later weaning. A formula of evaporated milk, corn syrup and a little water with egg yolk should be warmed and fed in a doll or baby bottle if necessary. A supplementary feeding often helps weak pups over the hump. Keep track of birth weights, and take weekly readings thereafter for an accurate record of the pups' growth and health.

After the puppies have arrived, take the mother outside for a walk and drink, and then leave her to take care of them. She will probably not want to stay away more than a minute or two for the first few weeks. Be sure to keep water available at all times, and feed her milk or broth frequently, as she needs liquids to produce milk. Encourage her to eat by giving her her favorite foods, until she asks for food of her own accord. She will soon develop a ravenous appetite and should have at least two large meals a day, with dry food available in addition.

Prepare a warm place to put the puppies to keep them dry and help them to a good start in life. You can use a cardboard box in which you put an electric heating pad or hot water bottle covered with flannel. Set the box near the mother so that she can see her puppies. She will usually allow you to help, but don't take the puppies out of sight. Let her handle things if your interference seems to make her nervous.

Be sure that all the puppies are getting enough to eat. If the mother sits or stands instead of lying still to nurse, the probable cause is scratching from the puppies' nails. You can remedy this by clipping them, as you do hers. Manicure scissors will do for these tiny claws.

Some breeders advise disposing of the smaller or weaker pups in a large litter, since the mother has trouble in handling more than six or seven. But you can help her out by preparing an extra puppy box or basket. Leave half the litter with the mother and the other half in a warm place, changing off at two-hour intervals at first. Later you may change the pups less frequently, leaving them all together except during the day. Try supplementary feeding, too; as soon as their eyes open, at about two weeks, they will lap from a dish, anyway.

WEANING THE PUPPIES

The puppies should normally be completely weaned at five weeks, although you start to feed them at three weeks. They will find it easier to lap semi-solid food than to drink milk at first, so mix baby cereal with whole or evaporated milk, warmed to body temperature, and offer it to the puppies in a saucer. Until they learn to lap, it is best to feed one or two at a time, because they are more likely to walk into it than to eat. Hold the saucer at chin level, and let them gather around, keeping paws out of the dish. A damp sponge afterward prevents most of the cereal from sticking to their skin if the mother doesn't clean them up. Once they have gotten the idea, broth or babies' meat soup may be alternated with milk, and you can start them on finely chopped meat. At four weeks they will eat four meals a day, and soon do without their mother entirely. Don't have water with them all the time; at this age everything is to play with and they will use it as a wading pool. They can drink all they need if it is offered several times a day, after meals.

As the puppies grow up the mother will go into the pen only to nurse them, first sitting up and then standing. To dry her up completely, keep her away from the puppies for longer periods; after a few days of part-time nursing she can stay away for still longer periods, and then completely. The little milk left will be resorbed.

7. Showing Your Basset

You probably think that your pet Basset is the best in the country and possibly in the world, but before you enter the highly competitive world of the show, get some unbiased expert opinions. Compare your dog against standards below. If a Basset club in your vicinity is holding a match show, enter your dog and see what the judges think of him. Match shows are rather informal shows held by dog clubs. There is a small entry fee, usually one dollar. These shows give you and your dog the feeling of the show ring and give you the chance to have your dog judged against others in his class. If he places in a few match shows, then you might begin seriously considering the big-time shows. Visit a few as a spectator first and make careful mental notes of what is required of the handlers and the dogs. Watch how the experienced handlers manage their dogs to bring out their best points. See how they use pieces of liver to "bait" the dogs and keep them alert in the ring. If experts think your dog has the qualities to make a champion, you might want to hire a professional handler to show him.

The Basset owner is in a good position at dog shows. Generally there are comparatively few Bassets entered in any show, and so there is a better chance of ending up with a ribbon or trophy if your dog has the necessary qualities.

STANDARDS FOR THE BREED

HEAD: The head should be large, the skull narrow and of good length, the peak very fully developed. The head should be free from any appearance of, or inclination to, cheek bumps. It is most perfect when it resembles the head of a Bloodhound, with heavy flews and forehead wrinkled to the eyes. The expression when sitting or when still should be very sad, full of reposeful dignity. The entire head should be covered with loose skin—so loose that when the hound brings his nose to the ground the skin over the head and cheeks should fall forward and wrinkle perceptibly.

JAWS: The nose itself should be strong and free from snipiness (too sharply pointed, weak muzzle), and the teeth of the upper and lower jaws should meet. A pig-jawed hound or one that is underhung is distinctly objectionable.

EARS: The ears are very long, and when drawn forward they fold well over the nose. They are set on the head as low as possible and hang loose like folds of drapery, the ends curling inward. The texture is thin and velvety.

EYES: The eyes should be deeply sunken, showing a prominent haw (red membrane inside the lower eyelid). They should be dark brown in color.

NECK AND SHOULDERS: The neck should be powerful, with heavy dewlaps set on sloping shoulders.

FORELEGS: The forelegs should be short, very powerful, very heavy in bone, close-fitting to the chest, with crooked knee and wrinkled ankle, ending in massive paws. A hound must not be "out at the elbow," a bad fault.

FEET: The dog must stand perfectly sound and true on his feet, which should be thick and massive. The weight of the forepart of the body should be borne equally by each toe of the forefeet so far as it is compatible with the crook of the legs. Unsoundness in legs or feet will absolutely disqualify a hound from taking a prize.

CHEST AND BODY: The chest should be deep and full. The body should be long and low and well-ribbed. Slackness of loin, flat sides and a roach or razor back are all bad faults.

HOCKS: Hocks are the joints bending inward in the hind legs, corresponding to the human ankle. A hound should not be straight on his hocks, nor should he measure more over his quarters than he does at his shoulders. Cowhocks, straight hocks or weak hocks are all bad faults.

QUARTERS: The quarters should be full of muscle, which stands out so that the dog from behind has a round, barrel-like appearance with quarters round as an apple. He should be what is known as a "good dog to follow" and when trotting away from you, his hocks should bend well, and he should move true all around.

STERN: The stern is coarse underneath, and carried "gaily" in hound fashion.

COAT: The coat should be similar to that of the Foxhound, not too fine and not too coarse, but yet of sufficient strength to be of use in bad weather. The skin should be loose and elastic.

COLOR: Any recognized Foxhound color is acceptable, and only in the closest competition should the color of a hound have any bearing on a judge's decision.

Well, how does your Basset shape up to these standards? Remember that the standards set an ideal for which breeders aim. Even the top-ranking dogs of the world do not rate 100 per cent, and different judges rate dogs differently.

You'll find out all you need to know about shows if you write to the American Kennel Club, 221 Fourth Avenue, New York 3, New York, and ask for their free pamphlet "Rules Applying to Registration and Dog Shows."

ADVANCE PREPARATION

Before you go to a show your dog should be trained to gait at a trot beside you, with head up and in a straight line. In the ring you will have to gait around the edge with other dogs and then individually up and down the center runner. In addition the dog must stand for examination by the judge, who will look at him closely and feel his head and body structure. He should be taught to stand squarely, hind feet slightly back, head up on the alert. He must hold the pose when you place his feet and show animation for a piece of boiled liver in your hand or a toy mouse thrown in front of you.

Showing requires practice training sessions in advance. Get a friend to act as judge and set the dog up and "show" him for a few minutes every day.

Fortunately, the Basset requires little special grooming for his show appearance. Brush him, see that his nails are trimmed, and you're all set.

The day before the show, pack your kit. You will want to take a water dish and bottle of water for your dog (so that he won't be affected by a change in drinking water, and you won't have to go look for it). A chain or leash to fasten him to the bench, or stall, where he must remain during the show, and a show lead should be included, as well as grooming tools. The show lead is a thin nylon or cord collar and leash combined, which doesn't detract from the dog's appearance as much as a clumsier chain and lead. Also put in the identification ticket sent by the show superintendent, noting the time you must be there and the place where the show will be held, as well as the time of judging.

THE DAY OF THE SHOW

Don't feed your dog the morning of the show, or give him at most a light meal. He will be more comfortable in the car on the way, and will show more enthusiastically. When you arrive at the show grounds an official veterinarian will check your dog for health, and then you should find his bench and settle him there. Locate the ring where Bassets will be judged, take the dog to the exercise ring to relieve himself, and give him a small drink of water. After a final grooming, you have only to wait until your class is called. It is your responsibility to be at the ring at the proper time.

Then, as you step into the ring, try to keep your knees from rattling too loudly. Before you realize it you'll be out again, perhaps back with the winners for more judging and finally — with luck — it will be all over and you'll have a ribbon and an armful of silver trophies. And a very wonderful dog!